C000164224

It all star conversation

Carolyn Williams

Carolyn Williams

Carolyn Williams

Published by
Chipmunkapublishing
United Kingdom

http://www.chipmunkapublishing.com

Dedicated to Emma and Rhys

Carolyn Williams

It all starts with a conversation
Carolyn Williams

Conversations that matter

Why do conversations matter?

` ` We can be wise only together'.
The ripple effect – our energy is our contribution.
Conversations that matter help us share our
knowledge and discover new opportunities for action.
Conversation is action, it's the wellspring from which
relationships and trust are generated and informed
decisions grow.

We want to talk together about things that matter to
us. This is what gives satisfaction and meaning to
life. As we talk together we are able to access a
greater wisdom that is found only in the collective
around questions that matter. We can restore hope
to the future.

Feeling this affirmation 'Be fearless in the pursuit of
what sets your soul on fire', I went after my dream
and launched The Carolyn Williams Show in May
2020.

My purpose is to host conversations that touch the
heart of what a human being or being human
means. Cherishing and including diverse voices.
Never be afraid to do what's right.
Stand up, be real and more importantly speak up for
what you believe in.
Success is a result of loving what you do.

Trust that when you live by truth in service to others, people will be inspired to do the same. My show encourages interesting people to join me for a café style conversation. I dive deeper into these conversations when we develop a deeper understanding of who we are as we explore each story.

My biggest conversation happened when I enrolled in a person centred counselling course at Swansea University's health care unit in 1991. This course was a pilot course and the first of its kind in Swansea University. I was experiencing the breakup of a twenty one year old marriage. I saw this course as a time for me to develop my self-awareness and personal development skills.

For years being in an unhappy marriage I felt I had lost my personal identity while supporting my husband through his policing and rugby career.

I had lost my love for teaching, life drawing and fitness and for rugby. I lost touch with my school, college friends and family having moved homes so many times. There was no time for me to grow other than as a wife and mother to two very different children. Building a home life, love, security and education was my priority. Most of my time in the first fourteen years of marriage was spent resettling my two children into new homes and new schools. The majority of police accommodation around the mid-seventies was abysmal. Every move we made I would have to clean, help repair and redecorate each house to make it feel like a home. My ex-husbands detective career took us to some really challenging places during the late seventies and eighties. During our third move to Baglan, my son was born. Bringing up two very gifted children in police accommodation became more and more difficult. The challenges we all faced chipped away at our health and happiness.

During our fourth move I deliberately started making fundamental changes. I started promoting adult fitness education evening classes as the fitness industry was booming. My main focus was providing fun fitness to music classes for adults. This helped me integrate my training while settling my two children into the local schools and the community. This conscious decision worked.

I knew I needed to retrain as a fitness professional to up my standard of teaching. It also gave me the courage to take a hard look at myself.

I kept repeating the well-known academic quote. The bible teaches us that personal change starts with truth.

'It is the truth that sets you free'.

My truth was at a time in the mid-eighties and nineties when being a divorcee carried a stigma. Financially you were at the bottom of the banking, housing, religious and socially accepted ladder.

As a divorcee my married friends disappeared. Very few family or friends felt comfortable inviting me to functions. I now understand that feeling of being uncomfortable means personal growth. It was at this time I decided to sign up to the first pilot counselling course at the Heath Care Unit at Swansea University in 1991. That course took me on a long personal development journey discovering how to feel worthy and centred.

Some very personal and private conversations among the students on this first pilot 'person centred' course surfaced much of my own personal anguish and suffering.

What became obvious and cathartic was the fact 'we are all one'. We laugh, we cry and we want to be heard. Being heard above all else is therapy. We heal differently and at different times but we all want to be heard, loved and cherished.

Conversations are sources of natural wisdom. We are able to access a greater wisdom that is found only in the collective around questions that matter.

Asking the right questions is the key, the catalyst to shifting our stuck perceptions.

Collaborative conversations yield insights for new possibilities and action. In flow, work and life are reinvented with new meaning and possibilities.

During this chapter of my life I wanted more than anything to become a coach with a real human approach. On becoming a fitness professional I learnt 'calling for action' was a crucial tool for growth. I heard it again from my publisher Jason Pegler.

Today, as a host on The Carolyn Williams Show I create a safe open space, where the guest feels comfortable. Not an intrusive space, a space which is conducive for best thinking.

Creating a personal connection is a key element in creating a hospitable space. My intention is to provide a relaxed, hospitable space to nurture authentic conversations.

'Let's dare to be ourselves, for we do that better than anyone else can'. As a conscious host I provide a comfortable space which allows guests to feel:

Physically safe
Emotionally safe
Intellectually challenged
Excited about striking a chord with listeners confirming we are never alone.
Creating a live masterpiece

Observing the invisible conversation is a skill. It empowers a different and more meaningful conversation.

Ripples of silence allow us time for reflection. Talk is cheap and that's poor. I love creating a new history together, to let go of the past and embrace the future.

Conversations provide us the opportunity to do just that. I want to encourage more conversations that matter and fewer speeches that don't.

You are always going to need to give yourself a push. No one does this, only you can parent yourself. 'No one is coming to help you. You have to Do it'. Mel Robbins

You have to get up in the mornings, get ready to take on the day, find that job, choose a date, contribute something worthwhile to your community by giving back and being of service.

By facilitating a culture of dialogue it's a joy to discover the magic in the middle of a new conversation.

I have enjoyed so many categories of conversations over the years from a wide range of people that matter.

My enjoyment of exploring conversations started during the literary and debating society at Llandeilo Grammar School and at UWIC in Cardiff. These debating societies gave me the chance to socialise and become vocal. That enjoyment led me to represent my third year at my college union. I learnt that having a voice within a student union group became a stimulating and worthwhile position.

Shaped by my experiences in life I began to create a career pathway of my own. Qualifying as a teacher from UWIC in Cardiff, I quickly realised the way to win hearts, minds and bodies of school pupils was through their souls.

Music, culture, history and sport had always permeated through my home and grammar school days.

My early pastoral teaching days shaped my love for relating better and winning over the trust of pupils and parents.

Last night I smiled broadly with a grateful heart while watching the concluding episode of 'Slammed' on BBC2. This three-part series depicts the miserable decline of Welsh rugby, following the highs during the late sixties and early seventies highs. Studying to become a teacher at Cardiff College, Cyncoed during 1967-1970 I was privileged to see players like Gareth Edwards, Phil Bennet, Mervyn Davies, JPR Williams play at Cardiff Arms Park. I vividly remember admiring a mature student called Terry Cobner who joined our year late. During my first year I had to live in digs as the college hall residence list was full. Bonding with your year as a student was preferable. It took me longer to bond with my college peers.
Welsh rugby is a massive part of Welsh culture and history.
The Western Mail headlines during my teaching days highlighted the enormous costs in building the Principality stadium. Cardiff Opera House was also in need of its share of funding.
Anyone who has heard the Welsh National Anthem sung full throttle, before one of the biggest international games in Cardiff will get a sense of national pride in both music and rugby.
For me, the two disciplines are one. Coincidently, I was taught how to deliver the National Welsh Anthem in my music and choral lessons at grammar school. We would get a chance to rehearse this every 'away game' of hockey, netball and when competing at the Urdd Eisteddfods on the school coaches.
Like most Welsh rugby supporters I experienced the highs and lows of Welsh rugby under some great coaches.

Each coach brought a dash of magic to the mix. Some things worked brilliantly and some things badly.

Together, players and supporters staggered through some rollercoaster 'Grand Slam' emotions. I am not sure who first coined the phrase 'We are stronger together' but that would sum up the rise of Welsh rugby to the world cup stage we enjoy today.

That energy and impetus experienced at Cardiff College gave me a platform to venture onto a bigger stage.

I saw an advert in the local papers and magazine reaching out to teachers to get accredited in exercise education. The London Central YMCA training and development Department started an accredited teaching scheme in the late eighties. I felt in my zone listening to University heads of sport give presentations to us teachers.

That experience was trumped when I joined the international development education association.

This association hosted the best sporting presenters from the UK, USA and Australia.

They charged their audience with a brilliant mix of humour and intellectual information. The lectures were broken up with high intensity exercise classes. That was the blend that got me. I wanted a piece of that stage.

Watching an American presenter (not unlike the comedienne Ruby Wax) throw out playdough to the delegates was exhilarating.

Normally national exercise education presentations were strict and rigid. This idea of throwing out playdough to delegates was hugely novel and productive. It gave each person the opportunity to 'shape their lives'. That highly interactive exercise has stayed with me to this day.

Mentioning Ruby Wax, a few years ago my daughter invited me to her performance in The Swansea Grand Theatre. Ruby was promoting her book called

'How to be human'. She was joined on stage with a neuroscientist and a monk.

'A three way encounter' sounded like a joke but turned out to be the most intriguing, informative performance about our brain health and mindfulness. Ruby gave a highly interactive and brilliant witty performance raising mental health issues and its stigma in society. Using humour she gave us an insight into her upbringing, her relationship with her mother, her husband, family and her mental health issues.

Walking us through her history with mental illness and exploring the help offered by her friends, the neuroscientist and monk.

Graduating from teaching the teacher's exercise education course, I was thirsty for a new challenge. The challenge came in the shape of Ford Motor Company in Swansea and Bridgend. The educational department was advertising for a fitness professional to facilitate their fitness facilities. Motivating their large workforce took up my energy and focus.

Then in 2009 I joined an online network for entrepreneurs and small business owners called ecademy.com. It was the largest social media platform of its kind, founded by Thomas and Penny Power from Farnham.

At this point I had launched two small businesses and was looking for a supportive group to share my day to day workload experiences. Being a sole business owner and a divorcee was isolating and very challenging. I understood the need for autonomy and belonged to a like-minded group.

Conversations with bullies

I saw a similar pattern emerge in this network group where the strongest and loudest voices drowned out the committed contributors. Thomas Power asked me to become a black star. This involved responsibilities for posting social media content with a trusted 'duty of care' to fellow members.

I saw daily posts and threads highlight individual grievances. These grievances if unaddressed would drown out the rich contribution from some really creative members.

Emotional maturity is an essential skill when being a member of a large digital platform. Writing blogs online gave rise to some nasty cyber bullying and you were either flattened or refused to be intimidated. The horrible behaviour of junior school bullies would raise alarm bells seeing hateful behaviour in the online playground.

The Powers built a strong network of trusted Black Stars who empowered each other and grew as staunch advocates. Conversations within a boardroom and later mini boardrooms were some of the most enjoyable black star lunches hosted in London. Those conversations and connections have lasted to this day.

Launching my own Cardiff Boardroom in 2011

After attending London and Farnham boardrooms I launched my very own Cardiff Boardroom. This provided a welcoming venue for trusted members to meet. As the numbers were small I decided to host mini boardrooms at Miskin Manor, a listed building, hotel and health club, situated just outside Cardiff. During one of my invites to meet with a business coach, Kevin Watson, I was shown a copy of the book 'The World Café'. Reading this book made me realise I was building my own café style conversations, where professional and sporting people would join me over a drink to share their stories. Chatting to Miskin Manor Hotel and Spa owners Colin and Leah and now Amanda Rosenberg I began to feel its immense charm.

At a time when noise and information overload is at its most debilitating Miskin Manor delivers a charming respite for its guests to relax and recover. I would often escape the ugly side of corporate politics and enjoy a drink with friends and Colin as he continues to keep a watchful eye over the family business. I would promote my Cardiff boardroom members and guests on my website, LinkedIn and Facebook network platforms.

I hosted fascinating conversations with a Welsh BBC film producer, a S4C camera man. I met small business owners and the incredible Lions Head Coach, Warren Gatland. My conversation with Warren Gatland, then head coach for Wales Rugby Union turned out to be the most humbling and historic insight into a famous, global kiwi coach's life. My next conversation was with Welsh Member of Parliament Mr. Byron Davies, who successfully won a seat in Gower. My love for Gower took on a new meaning, learning more about his campaign to win this seat.

I would post these conversations on my websites and on the giant social media platforms under the banner 'Café style conversations'.

It was the birth of 'going live' that changed not only the media vehicle but the flavour and global scope for sharing marketing conversations and content.

Three years ago, two great friends, Jenn Walter and Cassandra Saquing, both from American Real TV and fellow online coaches, encouraged me to launch The Carolyn Williams tribe, a group on Facebook and Instagram.

I asked myself this question:

'Do I have the courage and stamina to host The Carolyn Williams Show with a supportive group of online professionals and continue to walk the distance?'

My answer was: 'We are all energy. And as a coach to harness more energy with fun worldly contributors we become stronger.

Contributions foster a sense of community. Asking questions that matter travel through networks.

The Carolyn Williams Tribe has been renamed CW Global Sparks

See how this collective and supportive group have grown during the covid pandemic. My Carolyn Williams group is for anyone who has the courage to walk the road ahead, moving through energy or emotional blocks that can keep us well and truly stuck.

Connections happen faster, ideas flow, we are more, do more, smile more, attract more and have more friends.

I continue to build on this amazing collective group, a mix of authors-illustrators, actors, dynamic photographers, property fixers, navigators, graphic, professionals and video designers, pensions and finance business owners and marketers.

Having this awesome experience and fun group means you can share your big dreams and where you can get help when you feel stuck. This helps you to shift your gears, to find your voice, to burst through your bubble blocks to become the awesome you are meant to be.

Conversations have not always been easy or enjoyable or two ways. I now understand the need for a supportive tribe when you're struggling to be heard above the constant internal chatter, media and family overwhelm.

I was brought up in a very strict welsh home, the youngest of three children. My dad would dominate our conversations.

He was a youth leader for South Wales post WW2. He would host several local, national and German dignitaries. His pioneering spirit sponsored by The Duke of Edinburgh award scheme, was to build bridges between the youth of South Wales and Southern Germany post WW2 during the sixties. His pioneering youth build continued for a good thirty years before he retired from being a further education officer, a non- stipendiary priest, and a justice of the peace. His calling for the ministry (a far cry from being a wartime pilot) was fulfilled and he was ordained, a reverend at St David's Cathedral in 1983.

I guess his influence during my formidable years was to pass on his indomitable pioneering spirit.
My spirit as a female growing up in a male dominated environment has since taken on a life of its own.

Asking good questions is key to having healthier conversations.

Rest and Reflect
Reflection gives us time and permission for personal growth.
We can ask ourselves open questions, difficult and searching questions for solutions.
We can rest and see how far we have absorbed and practised our new found knowledge.
We can see how much action we have taken following our new found and tested knowledge.
We can see how far we have come as individuals and as a collective re The Carolyn Williams Global Sparks.
We can give feedback to those people we have supported and helped.
'Asking questions that matter travel through networks'.

Dividing the skills category of both hosting a show and attracting a global community like my Carolyn Williams Global Sparks group is useful. Asking my guests good questions on The Carolyn Williams Show most times brings about a result.
It is my intention to ask good questions that help my guests reflect and experience those very special 'aha light bulb' moments. These moments are very individual and timing holds the key.

Communication skills and every day social greetings

Our everyday greeting in the UK is usually 'It's a nice day, shame about greetings following on from the weather goes like this...

How are you and your family?

Did you watch the six nation's rugby game on the weekend?

Since Covid19 the questions are more along the lines of the vaccination confirmation.

I note a person looks relieved when I tell them I've had 'the two plus booster jab'.

Since the restrictions, more visitors have travelled to Swansea and Gower. The customary greetings centre on questions like:

Which beaches are safe for swimming, paddle boarding, and surfing?

Where can we get a decent and reasonable car park and a coffee café?

Friends will usually ask about your health, work and sporting updates.

I've stopped asking about work satisfaction as most of my friends are unhappy at work. It was this unhappiness (and my own) that led me to start my freelance and sole business ownership in 1987/89.

In the nineties corporate work politics in Wales was being throttled by employees fighting for improved pay. There was and still is no such thing as equal pay for men and women. Teachers pay was forever the main topic in the staffroom during my teaching days in the seventies

My focus as a fitness professional was on improving and promoting wellbeing at work. Forever wanting to improve my standard of coaching I would look out for courses to develop my coaching status. This

focus led me to search out the best accredited
national teacher training courses available.

I have always valued my own personal health. My
brother became a doctor, having trained at St.
Mary's Paddington Hospital in the seventies. He
played rugby for his county, then Llanelli before
joining London Welsh, as a trainee doctor.

His sporting prowess and fitness awareness was
seconded by my sister, whose specialist subject was
Physical Education. I had always been competitive
but was unaware as to how competitive, until I
joined the London Central YMCA 'teaching the
teachers'. This was a teaching the teacher training
course that was based on the theory from both
Loughborough University and Brunel University in
the late eighties. This teacher training developmental
department based on Tottenham Court Road pushed
you to excel in your teaching delivery.

Those aspirations and self-development steps quickly
became personal. I took responsibility for teaching
adult fitness and Look after your-self classes. Today
Adult Look After Yourself health courses are called
self-care courses.

In my teaching experience I saw a lack of confidence
and self-esteem in tough city schools. If pupils and
adults had little support or guidance at home, it was
left to the school teachers to provide that pastoral
care.

Being married to a detective for twenty one years, I
had moved every two years. This was my learning
curve as a teacher, a mother and a wife. The social
negativity and small talk would drain me. Some
environments would add to that negativity. I would
use sport, music, art and networking as a catalyst to
live a better and more meaningful life.

Returning from London to Swansea after teacher
training courses I would read positive self-help and
self-development books. I made a conscious decision

to attend as many enterprising events and professional and business seminars as was possible. I made a conscious decision to look for positive signs and ask for professional sign posts that would give my teaching more meaning. Answers were corporate fitness ones. The corporate wellbeing territory had not been explored in the late eighties.

The challenge of becoming a service provider to a Welsh automotive company excited me. Welsh icons like Lynn 'the leap' Davies, continued to inspire me. Gaining his insights and experience of the commercial business was paramount. He became my corporate career referee.

Igniting sparks in someone empowers them. Sparking the flame takes two energies. The mental response aligning with an open heart response creates the shift.

I delivered a wellbeing service to Ford Motor Company in Bridgend, and previously Swansea for over thirty one years. That service came to an end when Bridgend Engine Plant closed its doors during covid19 September 2020.

During those learning times I had many, many conversations that would range from weight loss, muscle weight gain, suitable fitness and nutritional programmes, relationship issues, to stress management, mental health, suicide, loss of family members and jobs.

Fortunately my adult health education training, qualifying as a counsellor from Swansea University Health Care Unit and gaining a National Customer Care training award, alongside two members of the chamber of commerce, equipped me with the necessary communication skills.

My own personal experience over the years has taught me how to claim my power back

I coach clients on how to have empowering conversations

These conversations can be asking crucial questions, such as:
Asking for a pay rise
Asking for sickness recovery time and cover
Asking for extra job training
Asking for support during a family bereavement and stress related illnesses.
What was noticeable that employees, colleagues, friends and family members would not ask for help when experiencing mental ill health or suicidal issues? Most sufferers would go under the radar and suffer in silence. Paradoxically that is when conversations matter the most. Paradoxical thinking becomes a popular topic among writers and coaches. Today, I listened to a Welsh female doctor on the radio suggest raising taboo health matters like the menopause, prostrate issues was necessary for there to be better and quicker diagnoses made by our general practitioners.
Learning to have important conversations around rarely discussed health issues like anxiety, abuse, depression, suicide, cervical and prostate cancers, would improve matters. Asking the right questions to a consultant or surgeon is vital for clarity and appropriate treatment.
As a counsellor/life coach we learn people don't always need advice. Sometimes all they really need is a hand to hold, an ear to listen (active listening) and an open heart to understand them.
Active listening often responds to active management. Keeping physically, mentally and emotionally fit takes time and training. Selecting an

appropriate coach, a trusted mentor is crucial for recovery and healing.

A bonus is having a supportive tribe or group who help and cheer you on.

'Stoking the fire' happens when I host my monthly online community.

I can focus on entrepreneurs who are natural at:

Bridging: working outwardly

Or Bonding: working inwardly

A balance of both is preferable when attracting and influencing new CW Global spark members.

Personal outreach is key, pinpointing people who I share a purpose and core values with.

Tips when I start a conversation can be:

Asking such questions as:

Why are we coming together?

Who do we care about?

Who do you want to work with?

What do people want to work on?

One of our global entrepreneur sparks has gathered a group of like-minded people, who are doing a half marathon at night, to raise money for cancer research.

Another entrepreneur has just published a stunning logo for the new business start-up. My role as a group host and mentor is to choose creative people who can help each other bring about a result.

More probing questions can be:

What is the change people desire?

Who do you want to help?

What is the problem only my group can solve?

Gains

We can help solve problems given the right tools:

Turn pain into power.

Turn that fear into fuel

That disappointment into a win, never to come back feeling like this again.

My entrepreneur bridge

I've been conscious of creating a natural organic bridge when networking. I'd network either through sport, enterprise or through business networks since the late eighties. My passion for networking started during my fitness professional training seminars in London in the late eighties.

My own network has taken years to build. This physical entrepreneur and professional bridge has grown from South Wales to Bristol, to Swindon, to London, Europe, America, India, South Africa, Dubai and Israel.

To possess great instinctive and intuitive traits can be a game changer when working with and coaching groups.

Developing great communication skills

What does it take to become a great listener? Do you know how to help others discover, motivate, observe, monitor and reflect?

Learning about self-awareness

Self-awareness cultivates emotional maturity among members.

By becoming emotionally intelligent we accept responsibility and stop blaming others for your failures. Everything we want we can manifest.

We have to do the work to claim it!

We discover our best self through going within to find our inner strength and to make changes for a better life.

Behavioural activation therapy

Pictures we play in your head are powerful. Negative self-talk destroys personal growth and happiness. Mental ill health is compounded by a negative self-image and a constant negative inner chatter. Hosting open and honest positive conversations is a game changer for mental wellbeing.

Words we use daily become our thoughts. Choosing our words carefully we can remind ourselves when we are going through a tough time we can always choose how we see things again. We can all change things believing we have the answers. We just need a time of quiet reflection to become aware of our breathing quality to increase oxygen levels which calm our minds and lower our heart rates.

Being a really good friend to ourselves, we can remind ourselves that we are loveable.

'Life Loves Me' a book written by Louise Hay reminds us to repeat these affirming words 'I'm kind and wonderful'

Remember our awareness is unique and uniting.

An exercise we can try is to surround ourselves this coming week with awesome people who lift us up and support us.

If we want to start changing our life, we can start being the person we want to become.

The more we act like the person we want to become (even though we may not feel like it yet) the quicker we become them.

Here is an exercise you can write down in your journal

Describe to me what kind of person you want to become and the actions you're going to take today to start becoming them?

Sometimes the hardest thing to do is to start. Fear can consume us and allow doubts to creep in. I wrote a ten week online empowering course called 'Crush Your Fears' which starts with a checklist and key strategies on how to overcome our fears.

Crush your Fears

Once you have focused on who you want to be and learn the tools to crush those fears. You will be surprised how this experience builds confidence. Resistance is the debilitating niggling inner voice. By deciding to commit to joining the London Real TV 'Speak to Inspire' group, little did I know that being resistant was my biggest challenge.
To overcome the ongoing feelings of resistance to completing my social media lives, to choosing the speech topics, to working on my instant inspire message I was put through my paces and hoops by the founder, Brian Rose.
I quickly learnt it was futile to resist. Every coursework would have a 'but or I can't'.
Overcoming all of these conditioned learned behaviours and responses served to convince us of our humanness. What got us through the phases was the support from our group. People from all over the world from different backgrounds would step up

and carry you across the finishing line, if you froze or lost your words. Going live and giving a message that you personally believed in had to have credibility, authenticity, accountability and reliability. Statistics and proven data were key components of research for our speeches. Our 'instant inspire' message was the emotional hook on which the success of our delivery rested.

My personal experience of seeing the numbers of city homeless rise sharply was the subject matter for my speech.

The personal hang-ups I had for speaking in public were real. I would be overly anxious and end up having to have relaxation therapy and hydrotherapy to get through delivering speeches to business enterprises, and sixty second presentations every week when I was a member of the Swansea BNI and Chamber of Commerce.

Once I had qualified it wasn't long before I got down to writing a ten week 'Find Your Voice' course. My own difficult journey to London experiencing serious self-doubt and lack of confidence catapulted me to provide content tools and social media link examples for anyone wanting to stand up and find their voice.

Graduation day, December 17th, 2017 with Brian Rose – Our Mentor for our Speak To Inspire Group.

Above is proof of me achieving my 2017 Goal! I had set myself a difficult challenge to become a public speaker and to inspire others.

My personal achievement

As a young teenager, I visited Germany for the second time with my parents. My dad was a WW2 RAF pilot, and then went on to become a pioneering, regional Youth Leader, building relations with the youth of Southern Germany and the youth of South Wales post war.

It was during this visit I had a cycling accident. Cycling down a grade 9 hill, I misunderstood the European braking system. At some speed I went head first over the handlebars straight into very tough cobble stones. I had a concussion, a fractured jaw, a ripped mouth and most of my front teeth were knocked out.

Thankfully, I received excellent medical care in a brand new German hospital. This hospital excelled in modern and herbal medicine. As I suffered concussion I was not given general anaesthetic while the maxillofacial surgeon treated my injured jaw and mouth. My jaw was wired and my saved teeth were transplanted. I was then transferred to my local Swansea hospital for further maxillofacial treatment.

Post-accident, I suffered periodic post traumatic flashbacks and mandibular dysfunction. My migraines would render me unable to form words and my speech would be affected periodically. I did not ride a bike again until I was forty years old.

Being forty I was determined to maintain a certain level of fitness to be able to improve my strength and resilience. From being a qualified teacher and later a teaching the teacher self-employed professional I made the decision to have hypnotherapy, cranial therapy and counselling for this cycling trauma.

This decision was to help me overcome my debilitating migraines and speech difficulties. I wanted to become a successful 'teaching the teachers' fitness professional after qualifying in London.

The directors of this accredited course asked me to promote the first accredited fitness course for Wales. It was during this exciting phase in my life that I decided to train for a thirty seven mile Gower bike ride, a yearly event, raising funds for 'The British Heart Foundation'.

My second start up business was to provide a cyber café service to the local community in Swansea. Before starting this venture I attended the Swansea trade and industry business training to gain local business funding. I also enrolled for a Cambridge 'Information technology' qualification at Swansea College.

In 2000, I co-opened Uplands Online Cyber Café with my IT lecturer. That local community training service insight enticed me to join ecademy.com.

This online membership site was the largest social media platform founded by Thomas and Penny Power from Farnham in Surrey.

In 2008 blogging had become fashionably popular on social media. It was a time when my son, a soldier, was posted to Afghanistan. Editing and writing blogs was my release and distraction as a single parent. I created my Lifestyle Online brand with the support of business Wales. As a mother of a serving soldier I found the medium of blogging and later vlogging cathartic.

At this stage, being a sole trader, I was being asked to give regular business well-being presentations, to the chamber of commerce, BNI chapters, and business edutainment networks in London. I found giving business presentations to strangers and colleagues both physically and mentally tough. I would suffer severe tension and often seek remedial and holistic massage therapy.

In 2017, I saw an advert on Facebook with Brian Rose, Founder of London Real Academy, offering his "Speak to Inspire" course. I had secretly been determined to improve my speaking skills and confidence. I had no idea how this course would change my life forever.

Here I am in the picture above, graduating as a 'Speak to Inspire' speaker with Brian Rose, Founder of London Real Academy.

After qualifying I wrote an online training course called Finding Your Voice

My challenge was to ask my network if they were serious about finding their voice. I gave them tips to help them develop great habits and a mini 'find your voice' coaching bonus!

Great habit tips to kick-start this Year! These habits are highly effective and applicable to this new 2022 year even.

1. Follow your instinct and start writing down your 2022 Goals!
2. Self-Care. Be kind to yourself. 'As you think, so can you be'.
3. Be kind. The person you talk to mostly is yourself!
4. Talk to yourself, as you would your best friend.
5. Here is a reminder to you that food is medicine.
6. Rest and relaxation is essential to you feeling well.
7. Take weekly media diets. Put away your iPhone.
8. Switch off the television and any screen or tablet.

9. Move more. Choose regular walks in Nature
10. Do more of what you love

Following 'Crush Your Fears' I marketed this second course on Instagram and Facebook by posting a Find Your Voice CheckList
Here is a workbook exercise you can do before recording a live.
In this post I give tips on how to worry less, believe in yourself, attract what you desire, quieten the fear and anxiety that you feel and find your voice.... We all need to be better communicators. We can master unlocking our conditioned belief system. We all have that power within ourselves.

How to build your emotional hook
1. Finding a topic you're truly passionate about
2. Recall a time when you really struggled to work through to the other side.
3. Recall how you found your solution?
4. Become aware of your inner chatter- resistance
 5. Learn new habits on how to overcome our limiting self-beliefs
6. Take small steps to overcome your struggle and learn from it.

You're Call to Action:
1. How you get your audience to take action
2. Becoming fit, relaxed and healthy is a great visual example
3. Becoming vulnerable – What happens to us when we are vulnerable

Here is one of my first Finding Your Voice American clients.
'Find Your Voice' client Dannielle Ufland Westfield.
Three years later, Danielle has gone from strength to strength and hosts a live show every day to her own American Public audience.

Hello!

Here is a Danielle Ufland Westfield (pictured above), from Buffalo NY and her Day 2 workbook outlining a structure for 'Finding Your Voice!'

Finding your voice training -

In this email I mentor you on how to worry less, believe in yourself, attract what you desire, quieten the fear and anxiety that you feel and find your voice....

We all need to be better communicators. Unblocking your conditioned belief system We all have that power within ourselves.

How to build your emotional hook:

1. Finding a topic you're truly passionate about
2. A time when you really struggled to work through to the other side.
3. How did you find your solution?
4. Became aware of your inner chatter
5. Overcome your limiting self-beliefs
6. How you overcame your struggle and learnt from it.

Call to Action:

- How you get your audience to take action
- Becoming fit, relaxed and healthy is a great visual example
- Becoming vulnerable – What happens to me psychologically, visually, physically and spiritually when I don't eat clean foods?
- Tell a story about a negative time you went through (of when you were unhappy)
- Take your listeners / readers to the place where you overcame this and how you became more positive - happier.

Exercises:

Food is medicine. Soul foods - Nourish not punish. Learn to be kinder to your digestive system.

Spend time in nature. Make time to exercise your body to release your stresses and improve your endorphins.

Meditate. Let go of what no longer is needed to serve you. Be open to nourishing beginnings, a time to rest, restore and replenish.

When you overcome your victim story, it loses its power, and then you can transcend it and begin the *process of growth.*

Learn simple wholesome changes that nourish your health and mental well-being.

Consciousness Energy Method Awareness

Carolyn Williams **2019**

Entrepreneur and Founder of the Carolyn Williams Show. I speak to inspire and mentor you to find your voice. I write online training courses to bring out the ability and talent you are unable to see.
Swansea, Wales

Join me in creating new habits for 2019!

If you want to win a mini 'find your voice' coaching session, comment below on how I can help you quieten the fear and anxiety that you feel and how to find your voice? Also please post your comments on my Instagram and Facebook page.

Thank you,

Carolyn Williams
The Carolyn Williams Show

Creating New Habits

Journal

1. In the morning write down on one side of a sheet of paper five things that make you happy.
On the other side write down five things that bring you down
Focus on the things that make you happy and do more of them.
Exercise
2. Make sure you exercise after you have woken up to get your blood flowing.
You can go for a walk or visit your nearest gymnasium or join a class of struggling new office workers, new mums and overworked dads, even retired people. Improving how we move and circulate helps how we think and perform.
Our purpose is to grow and contribute.
Meditate
3. Learn how to let go of the constant niggles and worries. Enjoy seeing your speed of thoughts get slower and float away.
Breathing well is a crucial part of relaxing. Meditating and letting go.
Feel
4. When we feel our dreams and become the person we want to be in our dreams we deserve to celebrate.
Momentum
5. Focus on building momentum. Become intentional in fulfilling your dreams.

Celebrate Becoming a Host

Learn to celebrate your small steps and your small wins. They will become giant steps and giant wins. This celebration time can be a quiet time to rest and reflect on what has been accomplished and what might happen next?
Make time to reflect if you have achieved a goal, hit a milestone
And ask yourself the question? What is next?
Reflection time gives us a space for 'not knowing' and this gives us satisfaction and meaning to life.
Becoming a host
Ask yourself positive questions that empower
Who are you without a voice?
Where is your happy place?
What is your why?
Who inspires you?
Who do you aspire to be?
Learning to let go of negative questions we have room to focus on creating new and exciting adventures.

Switching up our mood first thing

Repeating affirmations like 'It's good to feel good today' helps us stop the constant negative chatter of 'I feel bad today'.
'I am healing today' as opposed to 'I am getting sick'.
Flicking the hate me switch can be done by a simple and quick body movement. As soon as a negative hateful inner voice says 'that's useless, that's shit' immediately raise your arm and do a 'high five' with

a smile, breathe in and out five times and chuckle. Repeating this BAT – behavioural activation therapy daily helps us to shift our mood. Doing this with a friend in person or over zoom lifts the mood.

Gaining clarity and learning tools to change bad habits you instinctively know what it is you love doing and want.

Your life and your direction is your responsibility.

Affirmations

Start your day by saying

'Today I will decide my future will be much brighter than my past

I am unique, dedicated, happy and confident

I can focus

I can create my future'

Science gives us evidence that making affirmative statements when you wake up and see yourself showing up, looking at yourself in the mirror celebrating who you are by giving yourself a 'high five' and smiling, you are pulling your dreams closer to you.

Jim Kwik, brain coach and New York Times best seller and author says 'When you know what to keep in mind you become more attentive and you absorb more information'.

It's remembering the name of someone you find hot is effortless

Ask yourself three questions:

How can I use it?

Why must I use it?

When will I use it?

Consistently lifting our moods and being disciplined we reap results. We become more productive.

Questions and Answers

As a founder of the Carolyn Williams global sparks group I get asked certain questions from my members. These might be:
What books, videos will help me overcome my inner critic and help change my thoughts?
What is your favourite meditation video?
Who inspires you?
My answers:
'The key for me has always been self-discipline. To create a better future for ourselves we have to see it, believe it, feel it and be in it daily.
By having a conversation we can focus on the things that spark our flames and keep us in flow.
Clarity happens when we talk about what we love doing. What matters to us, our causes and values ignite our passion, our flow
For better insights and data, I follow the late Wayne Dyer, Louise Hay, Doctor Joe Dispenza, Mel Robbins, Suzy Walker, Gabby Bernstein, Lewis Howes and Jeffrey Allen. Great presenters, authors and speakers can be found on YouTube, amazon and Mindvalley podcasts.
Reading and listening to great orators is a must for speakers. We gain momentum by listening, thinking and observing how to deliver great speeches. Some of us might even choose to facilitate a platform to shine a light on inspirational presenters.

My speaking journey

Wanting to express myself and reach a bigger audience took me to London Real Tv, having followed several Brian Rose interviews on YouTube and Facebook. Great television hosts and interviews

have always fascinated me. Staged managed interviews are purely for entertainment but interviews where the host provides a safe space for a guest to articulate their unique story is beautiful.
I watched top sporting stars, doctors, surgeons; psychologists, celebrities and incredible survivors all add meaning to their lives on the Brian Rose show.
I now deliberately go out of my way to invite someone to tune into their inner voice and become their own cheerleader.
The answers lie within. Freeing the bold spirit within, we feel more confident.

Story Telling

I truly believe there is a storyteller in each of us. Your story given the right mentor and exposure will inspire you to make the shift.
As a host and mentor on The Carolyn Williams Show I have seen guests make a big leap.
I invited a homeless man, who previously was a highly successful property developer on my Show. This conversation became so powerful video creator, Ian Moncrieff MacMillan and I edited five clips to capture his decline and fight to reconnect with his four children, being homeless experiencing an agonising time apart.
Another hugely overly busy business owner now spends quality time with his two daughters. After he appeared on my Show he wrote to let me know he had started a new career as a Spotify artist and a new life with a new significant other.
A popular female actor has gone on to star in numerous film series. Another one of my illustrious guests has retired from a mega-busy journalist job and is travelling in her bright coloured camper van.

A fellow social media presenter is now thinking of writing a few 'How To' e-books.

These are changes that my guests made, a few, before appearing on my show or as a result of several epiphanies and soul searching questions after my show.

Feeling confident hosting conversations that matter will connect you to the right people.

The best daily practice is to face the fear and then emerge from the other side. Doing the work and this practice is a sure way for your confidence to grow.

My story

Being different

When I look back on my Welsh primary school days I felt different and I was different from other school children. My father had become a pioneering Youth Leader post WW2, bridging the horrible gap between the youth of South Wales and Southern Germany. He forged tirelessly to raise funds through the late Duke of Edinburgh award scheme and local educational schemes. This funding meant that he was able to start youth exchanges between Germany and Wales. When we three children had been well behaved both at home and in school, we would be allowed to join my dad on a few of his trips. That journey was to London to Dover by rail across to Calais by boat and then to make our way to Southern Germany by train.

As a very young teenager these travels made me think and behave differently. Sadly like many different school children I was bullied for being different in school. Being completely cornered in my school playground one day changed my behaviour. That bullying incident made me determined to celebrate my difference and work hard to leave that school for a better one.

Thankfully, my high school was different. I focused on my school exams to become a well-rounded and travelled teenager. Being well liked or part of a gang was never my intention, being creative, a team player and different was. I enjoyed being different. I embraced it and found that being selected as Captain for school sport teams, literary debating societies and senior school prefect was my reward for my hard work.

I watched some of the world cup football games this year and saw three brilliant young players from different clubs get chosen to take penalty shots for England against Italy. The sudden call up and lack of warm up, plus global pressure resulted in these young players having no goals. What happened after this game was for the world to see. England lost to Italy after qualifying in a semi-final. The bullying and abusive behaviour of a minority against these young players quickly turned to pride and support from all corners of the U.K and beyond.

Being young and talented, bravely stepping up to play for such high stakes took courage and conviction. There is no doubt that these three beautiful players will come back better and stronger. All these major tournaments given the right coaching will turn skilled ambitious players into Ambassadors. Sport has its own code of conduct both on and off the field or stage. The sign of a great coach and mentor is to help players bounce back from major incidents.

This applied to my previous role as a corporate fitness coach at Bridgend Engine Plant Ford Motor Company's crossfit gymnasium. I wrote a gymnasium etiquette set of rules for corporate employees who used the Gym. This extensively refitted cross fit gym etiquette was a 'hit' and copied by outside private gymnasiums. My passion for sharing great etiquette and great vibes fuels my creative writing skills.

Experience tells you to enforce a code of conduct when managing a large facility. I always wanted to create a safe and healthy experience for users both inside and outside a gymnasium.

Attracting new members through energised marketing both online and offline is my strategy. Fostering gym etiquette becomes a healthy tool for all members to enjoy themselves. Respect for self is a great learning curve as you respect others.

My daily practice of smiling and how it expands my flow of energy

Smiling expands our energy reach. My meditation practice of smiling lifts and attracts more energy to you.
I encourage my group members to engage with each other and to support one another's ventures or projects. I also host a monthly online networking event which stimulates ideas and gives everyone a chance to step up and speak.

I post regular coaching tips to attract new clients and here are a few challenges I posted on social media during Lock down.

Coaching

Carolyn's vavavoom coaching

It needs glue to connect the dots for flow □

Imagine you being Lewis Hamilton in the driver's seat on his way to becoming Sports Personality of The Year □ He too has a skilled team and tribe behind him. You can have that too! If not now, WHEN?

Who are YOU? Can you answer that question honestly?

Have you been overwhelmed by circumstances beyond your control?
Can you get out of your own WAY?

Yes, you can.....with a trusted guide who can see the potential in you
How? Commit to quieting the noise and calming the mind.

1. Once you learn a new habit of meditating.

Becoming aware of how well you...

2. Breathe you will gain
3. Clarity of thought.
4. Your focus becomes laser sharp.

Tips on how to improve your breathing and meditation

My 7 Day Breathing Challenge
Day 7 Reset Sunday. Christmas Lock Down Langland Bay via Carolyn Williams

'Look Up, that's where the magic is,' preferably go outdoors (if possible) and look up at the skyline. This exercise is more important now during our Christmas Lock Down.

Here's your Sky delight, day 7 of a 7 day breathing exercise challenge kick-starting our Christmas and 2021 come back.

Focus on how you're breathing.
Is your breathing shallow?
Are you hyperventilating?
If yes, become aware of diaphragmatic breathing

Exercise

> Stand with legs astride, keep the knees soft (take a deep breath in) bringing both arms straight up overhead.
> Then lower arms to shoulder level.
> Bend both elbows and bring the palms together and rub them together to add warmth and energy.

Follow your fingers across your rib cage and then across your stomach and take a deep breath in. Are you breathing from your neck, chest or stomach?

*Become aware of using your diaphragm muscles to accommodate the inhalation and exhalation.

Thump your chest (like Tarzan) either side (between your shoulder blade and your sternum. You can make a gurgling noise like Tarzan; it stimulates your vagus nerve too!

The word "vagus" means wandering in Latin. This is a very appropriate name, as the vagus nerve is the longest cranial nerve. It runs all the way from the brain stem to part of the colon

> Take a deep breath in round your back (yoga cat move) and exhale and drop your back keeping your tail high. Repeat three times. (Good for your digestive tract)

> Place both your hands either side of your sternum or massage those chest muscles in a circular motion. Doing this daily helps to flush out mucus.

> Rub both palms together then place them over your heart. Breathe in love for the great work

your lungs do for you every day. Exhale and feel gratitude. Repeat three times.

'Peace around you starts with peace inside you'.

🩶 Enjoy feeling good.
Carolyn Williams ©

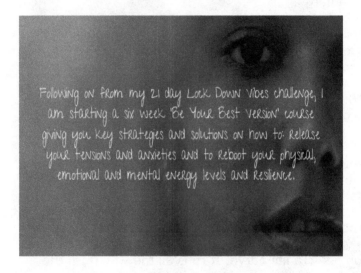

Following on from my 21 day Lock Down vibes challenge, I am starting a six week 'Be Your Best Version' course giving you key strategies and solutions on how to: Release your tensions and anxieties and to Reboot your physical, emotional and mental energy levels and Resilience.

I wrote 'Be your best version' a six week online course for New Year 2021.

The Best Way to be yourself

Knowing and experiencing your true unlimited self, energises every aspect of your life from the inside out. Our experience of ever-present awareness in meditation gives us that contact with our real self. But how are we to understand and sense our true self outside of meditation?

Start now. Start teaching the people you work with, what you're doing. Start being the light wherever you are. Continue to have so much fun along the way, even if you're not there yet. The joy you're having in bringing these principles to life will clearly guide you towards what it will look like in your career.

Be in it now.

This practice happened to me only last Wednesday, a lovely fellow congregation member who helps serve meals to our homeless in Swansea was rather quiet and reflective.

She is always quiet but that day she was very quiet. After a half hour I asked her if she felt well. She said she felt very well and carried on packing the meals. I checked her again and added 'you seem overly quiet today are you sure you are well?' Her reply astonished me. 'I feel 100% I've been meditating on the problems we see here'.

Three Ways to Start Achieving Your Dream Today

Take one little right action

"Just a lot of little right actions"

When we're really passionate about a new venture, we want to rush right into it.

When we do this, we can push ourselves too far, too fast. Instead, honour the transition.

Choose to see your day job as your personal venture capital in funding your dream. And start taking actions in your dreams that are doable.

Get rid of expectations

- If you want to write, write the first draft of a blog post.
- If you want to start a podcast, record an episode using whatever equipment you have available.
- If you want to make inspirational YouTube videos, set up your own channel.
- Even if you want to do a hundred different things... start with one little right action?

You don't build anything big overnight. And if you believe you need to do everything right now, I guarantee that will stop you from doing anything at all.

So go easy on yourself! Just take one 'little right action' at a time.

You will get into new energy

Forget about who might read your blog, listen to your podcast, and watch your videos.

If you want to host a podcast, record your first episode without expecting a single person to hear it.

Whatever you dream of doing, do it *just for the sake of doing it*?

Don't judge yourself

Self-judgement is the one thing that blocks you from doing what you want to do. Our ego voice loves to sneak in and say things like...

"Who do I think you are? I'm not qualified to do that."

The ego loves to pop up whenever we're learning something new.

You may think something like...

"I have to work to figure this out, so it must mean I'm bad at it. I'm making mistakes and it's not coming effortlessly, so it's just not meant to be."

Here's what to do when this happens...

Ask yourself who is judging you and why?

Write your answers in a journal and then write another column that says

'I am enough' 'I am amazing at what I do'

'I inspire others by what I do.' I know I was called to do this!

💜 Enjoy feeling good.
Carolyn Williams ©

And here I am focusing on writing my first book.

Building My Community

The Carolyn Williams Global Sparks group

Here is my brief chatty newsletter I sent to all my Global Sparks who have joined my Facebook group.

"I don't know what it's like where you are, but it's baking here!

It's 32C (which is 100 something silly in Fs).

I'm even "defrosting" my fridge by climbing into it.

Summer is definitely here!

This reminds me that August is summer playtime. I'm off to the beach - bucket and spade at the ready. So should YOU!

Please share what you're up to and any important news in the Facebook group. I'll be there all summer and sharing things like my son's wedding photographs (so excited)

Carolyn Williams

My hat created by Pippa Eastman millinery won't be quite so noticeable but there again...

I love how it's all coming together and how we're all connecting. The next online event gathering will be early September. I have something new I'll share with you nearer to the end of the summer. I think you'll like it.

See you in the group.

Love from me, Carolyn x

My Wedding Hat

My relationship with hats started with having to wear bonnets to church on Sundays. My father had become a lay preacher for the Church of Wales. Most Sundays I would attend church with my mum, brother and sister.

I managed to resist wearing a hat most weeks but would have to relent to wearing one during Easter and Christmas celebrations.

My fondest memory growing up was sliding the bonnet off my head onto the church floor. I would say my hair was far too silky for the hat to stay in place for more than an hour. This plea would usually work until it became acceptable that girls didn't have to wear hats in church.

The next time I wore a hat was to my brother's wedding. It wasn't a very large hat thank goodness. I was able to secure it on my head.

My sister wore a white fur hat to my wedding, as it was in December and freezing cold. That fur hat was a massive hit and was the last time for us sisters to conform to a dress code.

The decision to wear a hat came about again when my daughter got married. It was a very private ceremony followed by a very large marquee gathering in North Gower. As this was a very special Gower wedding in Fairy Hills, a stunning location the decision was made for me. A local photographer had been commissioned to take some very precious photographs.

My son was giving his sister away in full royal horse artillery sergeant's uniform. I had been asked to read Kipling's poem. It called out for a large brimmed hat that would hide my eyes when feeling emotional. It worked. I was so elated I could pull down the brim over my eyes, I wore it again the following morning to breakfast. It proved to be the very best hangover cover invented.

This month my son gets married in The King Arthur Hotel in Gower, to his lovely bride Zoe, a teacher and head of the art department in a private school. My son has decided to wear his full warrant officer uniform. As soon as he decided to wear his uniform he asked me if I was going to wear a hat. You guessed it; I now arranged a rather grand hat in keeping with this fabulous occasion.

I have been on the lookout for a suitable hat for some months. It was my daughter who mentioned there was a very clever millinery lady in Mumbles, called Pippa Eastman. She came highly recommended for her elaborate wedding and Ascot hats. It took me a good weekend to track her down. She had moved her workshop to her home. Pippa's workshop is now called 'The Hat House' situated on Argyle Street just off Oystermouth Road. The search was worth it and for more than one reason.

We had lived in Shrewsbury for most of my son's nursery years. He had been lucky enough to attend the Shrewsbury Public School for Boys nursery school. He had two great friends called Oliver and Richard, who were sons of two amazing house masters. This secondment, a detective post, was offered to my ex-husband and attached to a special branch.

I loved Shrewsbury. It was supposed to be an eighteen month post but we managed to stay longer. When it came to moving back to Swansea we decided to live in Sketty for both our children to attend Tycoch Schools. The Infant school had a very small school site and after a few difficult months, I made the decision to move my son to attend Christchurch School in Sandfields. It was the best decision for him. He stayed in Christchurch until he was eight years old. The school was situated off Argyle Street. You can imagine my surprise parking my car opposite Pippa Eastman's 'The Hat House' to find she lived on Argyle Street. Serendipity had brought me back to his Infant School area to choose a very special hat for my son's wedding.

As soon as I stepped into Pippa's workshop I felt at home in her creative bubble. She, like me, is very passionate about her work and customers. It took me all of five minutes being guided by her to pick the hat and colours for my outfit.

Gone was the highly self-conscious school girl who was made to wear a hat. This choice of hat was free and passionate. The floaty brim, layered with dusky pink and white feathers captured my imagination. My conversations with Pippa were instant, spontaneous and respectful. We both understood the dynamics of women wanting to glamorise for a particular occasion. What I have yet to ask her is 'Do male customers come to her for their hats'? I saw a very beautiful Drag Dj in a local bar. Seeing how immaculate her make-up, wig and dress sense was made me wonder if Pippa designed for Drag queens. I learnt later she does.

When you can have an open conversation like this you understand what it means to be comfortable with being uncomfortable.

Many people shy away from uncomfortable conversations. When you find the right person you can enjoy deeper, more meaningful ones.

Pippa and I got straight into where we were now in our professional career choices.

HMP in Swansea is yards from where Pippa lives. I explained I had taken up a part-time contract to help run a 24/7 activity rota to help inmates wean off substance abuse.

During our conversation we realised we knew a local artist friend who had tried to persuade Pippa to offer her artistic flare to prison inmates. Pippa decided to become self-employed millinery but had enjoyed taking art tuition.

In our conversation around the topic of art and craft I realised that I have always had a love for art, sport science and kinesiology.

Being gifted and happy in both mediums has enabled me to explore a wide range of skills and start-ups. Being actively creative has enabled me to find different ways of handling stressful and anxious periods in my life.

It seems I resort to photography and hiking to enjoy mindfulness activities. There is nothing kinder or calming than observing trees and oceans.

Studying their movement and inhabitants takes you into a much deeper state of calmness. Painting and taking photographs of ocean waves, surfers and paddle boarders is therapy.

It would seem Pippa and I share family values, a love of vibrant colours and the sea.

Pippa has become a very special part of my Global Spark family.

The Carolyn Williams Global Sparks

A much needed dose of humanity during a global COVID pandemic crisis.

We are all energy. To harness more energy with contributor's I decided to start the Carolyn Williams Global Sparks. See how this collaborative and supportive group has grown over three years. It's a group for anyone who has the courage to walk through and beyond energy blocks that keep us well and truly stuck.

My own experience of difficult and uncomfortable conversations around death, family relationships, religion, politics and social injustices help us understand each other. Humans are feeling beings that think. Not thinking beings that feel.

I'm blessed with the knack of bringing people together and coaxing out what's in the heart before trying to unwind what's in the head.

Having the right conversation at the right time may mean more in a person's life than anything. This is also true of reading the right book at the right time. I invited Suzy Walker, then Chief-Editor of the number one UK magazine, Psychologies, to my show to celebrate the first edition of a book she wrote called 'Making the Big Leap'. This book title jumped off the bookshelf in a London bookshop. This was a sign I needed to kick-start my new single life. I aligned this title with my passion for aeroplanes and the need to skydive. Fast forward to 2021 I have flown over Gower in a microlight but it's my son who has achieved his British, French and German wings parachuting, while serving in his Royal Horse Artillery and now Royal Artillery regiment.

Rhys (my son) parachuting with The Royal Horse Artillery in the French Alps.

These signs become pronounced for me during another transformation in another chapter of my life. I continue to build this amazing online community group where you can share your big dreams and where you can get help when you're feeling stuck and in a crisis. To be more, smile more and have more friends.

'True changes happen within leaving the outside as it is'.

Dalia Lama XIV

The need for love lies at the very foundation of human existence. We need a genuine sense of responsibility and a sincere concern for the welfare of others.

If someone speaks with human feelings we enjoy listening and respond accordingly.

The whole conversation becomes interesting, however unimportant the topic may be. Here lies the clue to hosting a conversation or giving a speech.

The emotional hook surfaces the lack of love or the presence of it. We humans thrive on affection and recognition. We grow by lifting and serving others.

In a community people talk, then they talk more. They learn more about each other and consider new ideas.

Brainstorming has been a personal monthly exercise for me since 2008.

We form deeper, more meaningful connections by sharing intimate moments in our lives.

In our community we share interesting topics. I continually update and invite new people into our group. It's a joy to be among fellow like-minded people who have so much to offer and who we can learn from.

I would never have met any of these beautiful sparks if it weren't for setting up The Carolyn Williams Show and The CW Global Sparks group during this COVID pandemic crisis.

Brainstorming with a connection is a human cantharis. A dose of what's real. The value of regular sustained conversations on topics concerning humanities and related fields are even more valuable in a non-academic setting.

A wide variety of voices and zoom calls open up conversations and avenues for anyone with a mobile or a computer. These conversations inspire a common ground.

We are social beings and thrive better when we connect with each other. We learn so much more by connecting the dots. There is much to be learned and experienced by moving forwards.

Conversations with key persons of influence

I came across Daniel Priestly owner and Founder of Dent
  (Make a dent in the universe)
In 2011 on Ecademy.com I met with Daniel Priestly online. In 2013 both Thomas and Penny Power were looking to sell their largest social media platform they had built up over a period of years. Daniel Priestly helped them to do just that. Daniel had written a book called 'Key Person of Influence'. KPI "Key Person of Influence' is an international best-selling book that gives an overview of how to become more visible, valuable and connected. More importantly, the book has inspired thousands of people to change the way they approach their career, their business and their personal brand. Daniel wrote a post earlier today that said …..'Dent Global (www.dent.global) has been selected as a finalist in The Lloyds Bank British Business Excellence Awards in two categories:
Business Enabler of the Year and The LDC Entrepreneur of the Year!'
He was giving a presentation at the O2 on Tottenham Court Road. I decided I would like to meet the man that was so influential and dynamic. His presentation did not disappoint. I travelled to London on a second occasion when he himself was launching his own initiative in bringing influential Black Stars together.
Daniel continues to influence entrepreneurs and business people on his oversubscribed 'how to get people lined up to do business with you' platform. During Lock Down he continued to host lives to encourage entrepreneurs to reset, reinvent and recover. His influence has been to boost energy and

drive in my mission to pursue hosting and mentoring on my own Show.

What he does is inspire and open up your thinking process of how you can attract more clients. To excel is to release all the potential that we keep hidden by our own selves, our own thinking.

Another key person of influence in conversation is Brian Rose, owner and founder of London Real. Again I was drawn to Brian's energy on Facebook as he rolled out his conversations with such a diverse group of global guests. His honest and open questioning inspired me to get in touch with him and enrol in one of his first 'speak to inspire' courses. When you become accountable and successful in calling your fellow group members to action, you are invited to visit London Real Studios, to give your final speech.

This experience was to change the shape of my life forever. Feeling larger than life I enjoy dealing the honest card first. I respected Brian for encouraging us to speak freely and to dig deep into our reason for speaking publicly. In my case this was an enlightening exercise. Being given permission to hold the spotlight and talk about what really matters to you. This opportunity was what I needed.

When you feel unheard as a child, a sibling, a wife and mother you value the opportunity to get up in front of an audience even if it's daunting at first. That opportunity came from key influential people. Those people are recognised in my prayers, my gratitude and my social media posts.

When I first moved back to Swansea from Shrewsbury I descended into a deep depression. My marriage was virtually hanging on a thread and the thought of returning to South Wales to start up yet another home became too painful for me.

My fears of all the obstacles we would have to face were right but my resolve and inner strength never wavered. I made the brave decision to buy our first house from inheritance money, given to me early by my late dad.

Hearing my genuine reasons for buying our first home, my dad agreed to help us resettle into life back in Swansea. In hindsight we did everything we could to paint over the ever increasing cracks in our marriage and numerous previous difficult police accommodations. Seeing cracked windows in our first available police house was a message I will never forget.

During our move back to Swansea from Shrewsbury I came across Don and Anne Lewis, both reverends at St. Mary's Church. St Mary's is Swansea's City's largest Church. Both Don and Anne welcomed us as a family in the early eighties. The late Don Lewis had become Dean of Swansea and the late Reverend Anne and their daughter Rachel, became the first female curates to be ordained in Brecon.

They were incredibly kind and would invite us to glamourous musical concerts at St. Marys. Andrew Lloyd Webber agreed to play alongside Sarah Brightman to raise money for the roof restoration. Seeing Andrew Lloyd Webber play a white grand piano in St. Mary's Church was the icing on the cake for me. At that point my late father was performing healing services at St. Mary's Church most Wednesdays. I felt at home in this beautifully restored and light Church. St Mary's had been heavily bombed during WW2 and part of restored Anne's Chapel was where I felt most at peace.

Don Lewis became my main referee for job applications and later posts. My second referee was another key person of influence, West Glamorgan's Industrial officer Robin Wheway. I met Robin as a Church warden at St Mary's. He had moved to Swansea, Mayals with his German wife Giselle and family from Cambridge. Robin helped run his father's engineering company in Cambridge before deciding to move his family to Swansea.

I have fond memories of these friendships and invites as we got to know one another. These regular socials proved to be my saving grace. I felt I could explore deeper conversations around education, my faith and life as a wife of a senior crime officer and mother to two growing teenagers. .

Moving from Shrewsbury was very sad and difficult for me. I'd worked hard to set up adult education fitness classes and enjoyed a hugely varied social network. The diverse conversations centred on family life, children's activities, sport, education and inner faith gave me a respite from serious crime. One of the most peaceful experiences was to join the Shrewsbury public school chapel services and later their master's suppers. Attending candle lit services was so ecclesiastical and healing.

Giving Business Presentations

Becoming self-employed in the late eighties I joined the West Wales Chamber of Commerce. Tim Raine was President, a legal land registry executive for the Welsh Development Agency in Cardiff. Tim was one of the first presidents to ask me to give a presentation to the Chamber of Commerce in Swansea. On reflection that invite was the first to motivate me to become a better presenter. Tim asked me to do another follow up 'away day' presentation for the Welsh Development Agency in Cardiff.

Tim suggested my content should be fun, educational and entertaining. – Edutainment. I chose body language and recognising personality traits among our fellow business colleagues. My main intention was to encourage movement and interaction between employees and executives. I divided the various personality groups into activities which meant they could choose singing, poetry, dancing and drama categories. Members of each group could mime, act, dance or sing their company's slogan, having decided which category they were best suited to.

I was well prepared with overhead slides and music to warm the participants up before giving their performances. I was no stranger to giving warm ups and knew of their importance before main performance events. Previously, I had been asked by Tony Elgie, Manager of Morfa Stadium, long before it was renamed The Liberty Stadium, to kick-start a celebrity athletic event, hosting Daley Thompson, following his Olympic gold medal. Daley was the main guest runner and there were a mix of Welsh rugby players, sporting Dragons and athletes attending.

Physically warming up sporting members before an event was nerve racking but mentally warming executives, finance and administrators another. I guess I felt rather like 'David being thrown to the Lions'. This was the start of giving regular presentations and seminars on being fitter for business.

A very enjoyable presentation I recall was giving the importance of well-being in business to The Women in Enterprise. This was a new network of Women in Enterprise in South Wales. I felt honoured and exhilarated by this invite. Learning about what colours would support my self-employed business image was a bonus. Being a firm believer in absorbing and applying new information I felt most productive delivering these personal growth presentations.

The birth of social media networking platforms

Visiting Chamber of Commerce events and delivering wellness in business presentations was a monthly event. During that period I opened my second start-up business with a co-owner. This second start up was a cyber training café located in the heart of student land in Uplands.

I instinctively knew that every business would be wise to embrace the internet. My extensive and often tiring experience, fronting a seven day week cyber training café meant I had no social life. This realisation prompted me to join a fast growing digital online networking platform called ecademy.com

This platform was founded and owned by Penny and Thomas Power. This digital network took me to London to study how best to use social media for business. Penny's book 'Know me' 'Like me' 'Follow me' was a huge influence in my decisions and direction. I decided to become a Speak to inspire speaker in 2017. In 2006/2008 I saw the rise of the growth mind set and influence the internet had for business and education. Social media was thriving. We were wise to respond, catch up, accept it or be left behind.

Social media friendships

It's no surprise to me that many of my guests on The Carolyn Williams Show are entrepreneurs I connected with from my days as a 'Black Star' on ecademy. Being a Black Star you understood the core values and importance of trust and interaction between business Global boardroom members.

My most exciting and memorable holiday was sailing in a Turkish gulet named Flaka Tarkin, along the Turkish coastline. Cornelis De Majer was a Dutch Black Star who lived in Holland and loved sailing. His ideal networking location was on board a sailing ship. Cornelis would invite fellow black stars to join him for a networking sailing trip around Amsterdam. He was one of my favourite Black Stars. His enthusiastic mentoring was summed up by his wise saying to me 'never to lose or dull my shine for anyone'. Maybe as a Dutchman he was able to relate how I would be put down for being Welsh and female. Cornelis was emotionally mature enough to see through the ridiculous jibes and comments that would whizz past my tiny ears during online events. It was at a time when I was going through a particularly worrying time. My son, then a Sergeant in the Royal Horse Artillery, was preparing for his second overseas tour in Afghanistan. I knew this to be a highly difficult tour for him and his regiment. Cornelis, himself a dad, understood my heightened anxiety and kindly invited me to sign up for a sailing holiday along the Turkish coastline with sixteen fellow Dutch guests.

The gullet's Turkish Captain Ali, was a regatta sailor and enjoyed 'chasing the wind' as he set sail very early every morning. Second day in and I was badly sea sick. Luckily, there were amazingly kind guests who looked after me called Willen Doolhof and Christine Doolhof Schaay, owners of Life Maxx equipment and their two friends. With their care I soon recovered my appetite and sea legs.

Cornelis understood this trip would lift my spirits. I did regain my energy for networking at sea. These incredible adventures shape who we are and who we become. I was so glad I'd connected with him and his fellow Dutch business friends. We bonded through a mix of autonomy and a sense of belonging. Little did I know my father's sailing

instructions on board our family sailing dinghy when I was growing up and my sailing teaching days in Treorci Comprehensive would prepare me for this networking sailing trip.
The Turkish seas were the most peaceful, warm and recharging vibes I have ever experienced.

Joining The Social Media Connective Dots

Some years ago in 2014 I wrote a blog (journaling)

'Write Your Own Story',

I was inspired by two authors.
One was a social media connection:
Lisa Cherry, wrote 'Conversations That Make a Difference'.
In her post she gave 'Top tips on focusing your writing creativity'.
She said ...

Allow yourself to be risky with your writing.
If you have something to say, say it, and say it well.
People like to read something challenging,
something different and something that speaks to them'.

Another Healing Light Radleigh Valentine wrote...

You are the designer of your destiny.
You are the author.
The pen is in your hand.

The outcome is whatever you choose'.

What or who inspires you to write?

Love from me.
Carolyn Williams

My Digital 'Connectivity' Connections

This first photo  was taken in 2011 at Morgan's Hotel here in Swansea. I promoted two start-ups. The first was super star 'leather and silver' Serbian Jewellery designer, living in Swansea.
Tanya Igic

My mini boardroom intentions were to promote and support local and global creative entrepreneurs. Setting up these mini-boardrooms in 2010 was so much fun and I could take the boardroom anywhere….

In 2010 I was able to support and promote

Steve Hall a business owner from Sheffield, living in Spain, cycling his way around all the U.K. football clubs to raise awareness for refugees.

2017 I studied and graduated December 17th as a speaker. 'Speak to Inspire' is an online training course with Brian Rose at London Real

In 2018 I hosted a savvy, social media crèche owner Cassandra Saquing who I had met online through Roger Brooks American Real on one of my first lives.

In May 2020 I launched The Carolyn Williams Show

In 2021 I hosted a long-time favourite Live a life you love' writer and former Psychologies magazine chief-editor Suzy Walker

Thankfully Facebook keeps me connected to all these beautiful Super Stars ⭐

My Enlightening Conversations

Since Lock Down and the Covid pandemic I started to have several conversations with Sam Aldred, the current curate for St Mary's Church. These conversations started after I first heard Sam speak. He is a natural speaker and commands you to listen to his 'call to action' sermons. That call to action was to encourage me to declutter my wardrobe and chest of drawers to donate clothes and offer my time to serve brunch to the homeless in Swansea.

The speech I wrote as my graduation speech for London Real TV studio in December 2017 was about the sharp rise in numbers of homeless people in our UK. Here was Sam and fellow worshippers delivering a sensible brunch service addressing the needs for the city homeless. Our previous Vicar, Ian Rees, had started a popular breakfast initiative along with the Church finance secretary, Allan Jeffries. Sam has extended this initiative by asking for more volunteers and donations to continue this initiative.

Julian and Dati Mamiso are two very special friends I've made over the past few years while coming to terms with being a single parent having an empty nest. Julian is an IVF consultant and a church warden at St Mary's

Dati, his wife having a business degree has invested in building new homes in Nigeria. Both have strong family work values and ethics. During some very difficult losses, my late brother and his late daughter Julian and Dati have comforted me. I asked Dati if she would join me serving the homeless on the Wednesday brunches. That was a smart move on my part as we formed a fun working partnership. Every Wednesday I would see younger men and women joining the hostel for homeless numbers. The numbers are increasing and like drug addiction there needs to be a national roll-out programme like https://changeahead.org founded by Mohsin Ravjani, one of my guests on The Carolyn Williams Show, to guide the most vulnerable from the time they find themselves on the street to taking part in re-skilling initiatives in the workplace.

Like all cities Swansea is doing its utmost to offer emergency accommodation and free meals to the vulnerable and homeless. We do see regulars daily and it's not uncommon to see local restaurants offer coffee and warm soup during freezing winter temperatures

I came across Mohsin Ravjani, the founder for change ahead organisation which is an App for homeless and vulnerable people on Instagram. He posted a photo meeting with Lakhi Singh, the property fixer in Mayfair. I messaged Mohsin and found his story highly inspiring. I invited him on The Carolyn Williams Show to tell us what happened to him when his property business and his marriage failed. He was the father to four gifted children. He found himself alone in his car homeless and contemplating suicide.

My question to him was to tell us his Why? From his answer my wizard video creator, Ian Moncrieff MacMillan and I created and edited five clips to break down Mohsin's journey. He articulates when he hit rock bottom and what it was that kept him from committing suicide. He wanted to use his expertise and experience to create an App that would tell vulnerable people where they could find emergency shelter, food, clothes and educational training programmes.

Mohsin continues to deliver his video presentations when invited, sharing his first-hand experience and solutions app. Thankfully he has reunited successfully with all his children who are university students. His story gave me much to work on and cascaded to St Mary's initiative for Swansea's homeless.

When you're comfortable in who you are, something interesting happens.

People feel really comfortable opening up to you.

I've spent thirty two years in and out of lecture halls, University sports halls, corporate class rooms and now on my Carolyn Williams Show online witnessing people bravely share their vulnerable stories with me.

And at times, I find that their stories are also mine.

Create Your Future

A creative person is motivated by the desire to achieve, not by the desire to beat others.

Over the last August 2021 weekend my son married his love Zoe on August bank holiday at the King Arthur Hotel in Gower. I had the privilege to wear my beautiful hat with dancing feathers designed by Pippa Eastman, on what turned out to be a truly sunny and stunning Saturday in August.

The bright warm sunshine shone across this truly awesome venue, The King Arthur Hotel, in Gower. My son Rhys is currently a Master Gunner, Warrant Officer 1 for The Royal Artillery, based in Wiltshire. His best man Lee Kennedy, a RCM based in Newcastle, travelled down with his partner Michelle. The wedding guests had travelled from London, Essex, Plymouth, Harrow and from across South Wales.

When they arrived I took the opportunity to take photographs of our family and friends. Many of Zoe's friends like herself are teachers in local schools. One friend is moving to teach in Cardiff shortly. I was able to relay to her my early teacher training days living in Cyncoed, Roath and later Cathedral Road in Cardiff. Cardiff has a unique energy to the City and part of my dissertation was to research the Cardiff Docks. My first teaching post was at Willows High, a comprehensive school in Splott, teaching a mixture of art, physical education and geography?

It's a rare privilege to greet so many beautiful people gathered in a perfect venue sharing so much love, laughter and conversations over two days soaking up the glorious Gower sunshine.

Preparing for this wedding has given me so much joy and focus. I had no idea how many beautiful conversations I had to enjoy greeting and chatting to all the guests. Watching both my adult children welcome and mingle with everyone both inside and outside the venue was pure magic.

Living in South Wales

Living in Wales you are never far from the sea, rivers or mountains. My grammar school in Llandeilo was built into the side of a hill. Our netball pitch was on a steep gradient; our hockey pitch was a farm field, full of cow pats and hoof holes. Sitting important O-level and A-level exams meant you were serenaded by farm animals from the mart, opposite the school. Learning to drive at the legal age of seventeen was either on a deserted airfield strip or behind tractors from Llandeilo market and lorry's going to Carmarthen markets or Llandebie cement works. When the motorways were extended in the late sixties and early seventies you were able to enjoy the feeling of endless open roads. Today however the increase of City traffic lights and maintenance bollards has surpassed farm animals on the road until you venture to Gower. Wild animals have right of way in Gower and visitors are welcomed by cows, horses, ducks, pheasants, rabbits and anything that happens to cross a road from common land.

Now that I live around the Marina basin I am able to see Swansea's Liberty stadium from my third floor kitchen window. Pre pandemic helicopters keep us company on bank holidays or during big match days. Swansea is built on a hill and you can get very fit by walking, jogging, running 10k's, cycling and triathlons.

The highlight of my summer is usually watching the Swansea air show and the red arrows. And before Covid the Radio One Breakfast weekend in Singleton Parks. Currently Swansea is building its biggest music arena just yards from where I live. Much has changed since I came to live in Swansea in the early seventies.

City noise and pollution levels have increased. The pandemic has brought about a wonderful respite from busy traffic and disappearing wildlife and woodland. I was able to hear birds singing and saw many rabbits darting in and out of their burrows on my daily walks. Exercising, taking photographs of the coastline and its ever changing skies is a natural mindfulness practice. That practice lowers blood pressure, heart rates and anxiety.

What we accept and face we conquer. In stillness I am aware I surrender during times of chaos and change. Learning to balance media information overload and chaos with discipline and focus helps to restore order. Time no longer exists when you let go and that's when new ideas come through in stillness. Losing ourselves to a larger conduit than ourselves allows us to experience new ideas. By learning to calm down, to regain clear thinking and focus we can find ourselves in balance, aligned and in flow.

In times of crises and chaos being creative and present helps us to align to transform and reinvent. Regaining mental and physical strength in stillness we allow ourselves to recover and restore our equilibrium.

'I have learnt silence from the talkative, toleration from the intolerant and kindness from the unkind: yet strange, I am ungrateful to those teachers'.
Kahil Gibran

The Carolyn Williams Show Global Sparks

New Seasons Catch Up

We all needed a summer break and I had a very special wedding to attend.

My son Rhys and his wife Zoe, got married at King Arthur Hotel, in Gower 28-08-2021

Photographer: **Pippa Carvell Photography**.

If you haven't seen my wedding hat already here it's called 'Carolyn'. I adored the dancing feathers and my daughter, Emma's hat was also created by the talented and much loved **Swansea Millinery, Pippa Eastman.**

Big plans I Small steps

It's time to get going...but sh** timing for me. I have surgery scheduled this Tuesday, September 21st and a few follow-up appointments that have rolled in around the next two weeks as I started planning activities for the group and preparing my shows.

 It's time to get our brains and brands working.

We all need a bit of clarity during this last quarter and drawing on the strengths of the group.

So...

What's your big goal?

What's your direction?

What's your big project?

What are the big steps you need to take?

What are the steps you can take now?

Don't be afraid to ask for help.....

What help do you need?

Who are you going to ask?

Also think about what connections do you need to accelerate your success?

How to make time for the things you really want- this is what I do (It works, try it!)

Write out five things that you really love to do.

Master laser focus

Practice quiet time

Starve your distractions

Feed our focus

Act like the person you want to become

Bring your future self to the present.

I suggest you answer some of the questions that you need to ask yourself

Do you have time today for the projects you would love to see progress on?

Things to do next are:

Select one task to focus on for the day.

Connect one to one with another group member or friend.

Put a post-up of what you're doing, what you need and how it's going etc. on the **CW Global Sparks** page.

I'm going to automagically post up questions while I am away. You will get a lot of value following along and adding your answers to each of them.

Think of it as a focus challenge..... And I'll mark your homework when I get back. :-)

And while I am at it, we should all do more shout outs for each other. When you feel comfortable and when it feels right, obviously.

Let's get laser focused on what you need.

What's your direction?

What's the immediate next step?

"It's difficult to stop someone who knows where (and why) they are going". Jim Kwik

Lastly, I am really looking forward to hosting the highly gifted Pippa Eastman Millinery in the New Year on **The Carolyn Williams Show**. I have a few exciting guests lined up for the spring.

See you in the group. Okay, get cracking!

Love from me, Carolyn x

Personal professional conversations while rehabilitating after two nasty falls

How lucky are we In Swansea?

It's been a time of health check-ups after two nasty falls in three years. I've had a cataract removed in my left eye and managed nerve pain and regained full range of movement with osteopathy and acupuncture.

On my seventieth Birthday month in March 2019 I slipped on an oily wet surface and in doing a half split I fractured my left high femur. This was the most painful and traumatic experience I've had to date. Unfortunately due to NHS delayed ambulance call times here in Swansea the called ambulance never arrived. It took another call from my brave daughter to my son, stationed in Wiltshire, to make arrangements to drive me to the accident and emergency department seven hours later. Needless to say I was not in a good place when I eventually got x-rayed. Two very kind and capable young orthopaedic doctors delivered their shock diagnosis and treatment. My choices were...a possible partial hip replacement, a full hip replacement or having oscillating screws to pin the high femur. Thankfully a clever orthopaedic surgeon opting for the latter operated on me two days after the accident. What followed has been a discovery of how best to rehabilitate for a full range of movement and muscular strength.

No sooner had the pandemic affected us all and the spacing restrictions were put in place. I fell again over broken walkway paving stones this time when visiting my local supermarket, in some pretty atrocious weather. This time I hit concrete slabs face first. Luckily local passers-by immediately came to my rescue and I was taken to the accident and emergency in a taxi.

I've not been able to trace the taxi driver, called Terry to thank him.
Both he and a very calm young supervisor, called Will, have restored my faith in humanity.

The pandemic has stopped hip fracture and leg rehabilitation progress for me and countless others. Being the spirited woman I am, this did not deter me. I took full advantage of our exercise hours to look for alternative pathways to improve my skeletal and muscular mobility. I posted regular exercise challenges both mentally, physically and emotionally for myself and to support my networks so that we could keep as active as possible.

Much indeed is owed to so many NHS doctors, nurses, paramedics, and cleaners and indeed taxis delivery drivers and all supermarket workers for keeping our food shelves stocked.

A special mention goes to:

My local General Practitioners, my consultants and

Simon Webborn Swansea Clinic
Limin Zhu Swansea Chinese Natural Medicine Clinic
Sebnem Onal Mumbles Dental Spa
Three favourite Swansea Gems.
Without the skills and consistent professionalism of these practitioner's throughout the pandemic I would

most certainly be struggling and in a great deal of pain.

It always starts with a conversation

During the autumn I hosted a group of inspirational New Women Entrepreneurs on The Carolyn Williams Show

This group of beautiful women was kick-started by Sonia Lambert, a witty spark among our CW Global Sparks

We chatted about their fun shine night half-marathon which turned out to be a sightseeing/ walking / running tour through London, raising funds for cancer research UK. #shinenightwalk

> We talked individually about our personal experience of cancer among our close family members

> You can find out more about their night time adventures on Facebook and on my YouTube channel.

You can also subscribe to my YouTube channel here: https://youtube.com/c/CarolynWilliamsBreathing4Business

Love from me Carolyn Williams

It all starts with a conversation Carolyn Williams

Sonia Lambert 2021

Optimistic October

Here is my conversation during Optimistic October 2021 to inspire you, if you feel hesitant to put your trainers on and participate in a spectacular fund raising event.

I was privileged to host four beautiful souls who shared their experiences of doing their first 'shine night walk' , a half-marathon through London. This event was to raise much needed funds for Cancer Research UK

Sonia Lambert a loveable and witty member of CW Global Sparks founded NexWomen Entrepreneurs Sonia encouraged fellow NexWomen Entrepreneurs, the gorgeous Khadine Sinclair Maxine Grimes Marcia Grimes to do a half-marathon through London at night time.

Listen to their individual stories about their loss of mums, dads, grandmothers, grandfathers, aunts and uncles, friends to cancer and how coming together empowered them to experience a joyous sparkly night-time walk.

Hear why these gorgeous ladies decided to do a half marathon at night time. Where they live and work and what makes them get out of bed in the mornings. I'm excited to add them to our Global Sparks Gallery.

It all starts with a conversation Carolyn Williams

Let's talk about this...

Books & coaches I follow and subscribe to on social media and here on Facebook

Mel Robbins The High Five Habit 🖐
Gabby Bernstein Happy Days
Jim Kwik Limitless
Simon Sinek Start With Why
Suzy Walker Making The Big Leap
Franklin Levinson Trust 'N Horses

Which writers do you follow and subscribe to?
Love from me. Carolyn Williams

Building Confidence

How true is this quote ...reposting from 2016?
'Keep your eyes open and your feet 🦶moving forward. You'll find what you need'?

Four weeks post eye surgery I am able to open my eyes and see better. Moving forward is both psychological and physical. New York's bestselling author and presenter Mel Robbins advocates starting our day by doing a 'high five' to ourselves.. in the bathroom mirror. 🪞

Mel writes

Let's normalise...

Asking for what we need.

Going back to school after 40

Living a life that's authentically yours

Getting divorced if you are unhappy

Staying single if you're happy

Not wanting to have kids

Moving if you're tired of where you live.

You should never feel guilty for doing what's best for YOU

What do you think should be normalised?

I've ticked Yes to every one of these boxes Mel

November Sea therapy.

My body is healing. With my right knee 'rock tape' I managed to capture these Langland Bay 'surfing vibes' plus a hot chocolate (courtesy of <u>Surfside Cafe (official site)</u> ....

Carolyn Williams

Here are my creative I rustic I scenic I
photographers conversations

With <u>Robert Zarywacz</u> <u>Neil Holman</u> <u>Carolyn Seager</u> ...

<u>Robert Zarywacz</u> Spring Nourishment

It all starts with a conversation Carolyn Williams

Neil Holman Dragons Breath. Brecon Beacons

Dragons Breath

Carolyn Seager Pobbles Bay, Gower

A Ceri Hurlow photo  Llyn-Y- Fan

Next up ….all being well, a trip away in the sun.

Here is a picture of how I'd like to shape my future.

To feel the warmth of the sun and surround myself by people who care for each other
.
I'm enjoying comments coming in from across the pond in the USA from Jenn Walter and Nora Bontrager in response to my coaching / mentoring programme post today.

Listening to the inspirational conversations from Mel Robbins across the media platforms as she aspires to become the No 1 podcaster, I agree when she says… 'At any moment you can choose to change'

I'd add ... 'You just have to set your compass the way you want your life to look like ...every morning.

The mornings can be the toughest to start switching up the vibes. I'm doing it. Are you?

My inspirational flight to Gran Canaria

Thank you to all the beautiful staff at the Seaside Sandy Beach Hotel
I enjoyed a wonderful (overdue) pre-Christmas holiday in a warm and friendly location in Gran Canaria suggested by my loving son Rhys.

My daughter Emma made sure I had my combined Christmas presents
(Travelling luggage) early for the flight.

I was so well looked after by everyone at Seaside Sandy Beach Hotel from Guasi, the cleaner to Fatima, the Bar Manager to Florencia Cruz, a Kinesiologist/Reflexologist and Physiotherapist from Argentina

And Paco, Francesco pictured below, who was 'front of House'
Paco and Dominic made sure we all remained safe and well by wearing our masks.

Suzanne, the hotel hairdresser cut my hair.

I was lucky enough to meet the Sub Director, Eva Karg for this wonderful chain of hotels. Eva is a smart lady, directing a great team of men and women giving excellent customer service.

My photos Christmas vibes at The Seaside Sandy
Beach Hotel, Playa Del Inglés Gran Canarias

THE VOICE

There is a voice inside of you
That whispers all day long,
"I feel that this is right for me,
I know that *this* is wrong."
No teacher, preacher, parent, friend
Or wise man can decide
What's right for you—just listen to
The voice that speaks inside.

Hi! My name is Carolyn 😊

My question to you is …

Who would you be without a voice?

💜 It's so easy to be overwhelmed and drowned out by the constant noise and information on the news.

💜 It's so easy to be drowned out during family and friends conversations and worse still arguments.

💜 Have you experienced shutting down when you are in a room full of loud men and women?

💜 Have you ever wanted to scream out in frustration to say 'Hey! Listen to me I have the solution'.

🟣 I've experienced all of the above during an era when you were conditioned by an elder who said 'Girls are meant to be seen not heard'.

Today, I use my voice to help others find their own voice.

Work on You for You

Coaching to feel a deeper connection to you

You actually matter

Believe in the miracle you are. Treat yourself with kindness.

When you are able to be seen, to be heard, to be accepted and celebrated for the unique individual you are, you start fulfilling your needs.

Yes, I help both men and women see with their heart. If you feel stuck I provide tools that show you how to come home to who you are. I hear your needs and give you a secure space to grow and learn.

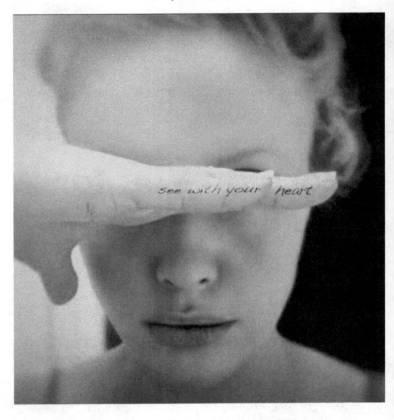

Photo via Savvy Raj a professional connection

'When you have a negative thought, catch the thought.

Identify what thought always takes you down?

That thought is poison. Catch it!

Replace this thought. Break the thought by saying 'I am not thinking that thought'. Move to high-Five yourself in the mirror'. Mel Robbins

I'd add when you see yourself high fiving in the mirror add your smile

Being accepted and celebrated makes you feel extraordinarily unstoppable.

I have coached people through loss, lack of self-worth and lack of confidence, emotional blockage and lack of energy.

Knowing we need support from other entrepreneurs I built my CW Global Sparks group. These individuals are the most loving, gifted human beings I've come across. Some are professionals, entrepreneurs, speakers, authors and some are serial entrepreneurs who can support you.

What if everything you wrote on your daily list came up trumps.

How would it make you feel to give out your message to a select audience?

I feel celebrated receiving an invite from two amazing entrepreneurs, Anand Raj and Preety Uzlain who grow their story of providing global supported college programmes for entrepreneurs of the future from India
This event at a government arts college in Coimbatore in India kick-starts week February 21st - 25th 2022

Branded Club Inspiring Millions Carolyn Williams is a guest celebrating this event week Feb 21st-25th 2022 in Coimbatore with Anandaraj Anandaraj and Preety Uzlain

Connection – Compassion – Empathy

Here is your call to action...

These are decisions you can make

If you feel ready for me to mentor you on my hourly or daily fee coaching programme e-mail me directly to <u>carolyn@carolynwilliams.wales</u> telling me about your why and your happy place and how you, your product or service improves people's lives and makes a difference'

You will learn simple daily techniques to say to yourself
'It will work', 'It'll happen', and 'I can make it happen' 'I'm in'.

If you feel ready to tell your story or give your message email me directly to <u>carolyn@carolynwilliams.wales</u> telling me how you, your product or service makes a difference to you, your family, your friends, and your community.

I will then send you The Carolyn Williams Show guidelines

Hello
My show is about having a two way conversation. Looking at what makes you get out of bed in the mornings. What makes you Tik Tok, your journey, your highs, your lows and your core values?
Here are My Show guidelines.
Welcome to The Carolyn Williams Show - 'interesting people with interesting stories'.
'Only you can tell your story'

Our Discussion length of time is 30 minutes
Here are a few points to explore:
Who are you?
What gets you up in the morning?
What is the first thing you say to yourself when you get up?
Which Digital entrepreneur are you? Signature, Spotlight or Starter?
Who is the Man/Woman behind his service and his brand?
Tell us which audience benefits from your work and service?
What is your Why?
Do you believe you can create your future?
Name 3 superstars / serial entrepreneurs, who inspire you or who you aspire to be?
Which audience are you targeting?
Where is your 'Happy Place?'
Coaching and illuminating promotional fees can be paid directly to me.
This covers my time and promotional CWS banner ads used to broadcast and illuminate your skills to The Carolyn Williams Global Sparks and YouTube.
Guests can also pay from PayPal
to carolyn@carolynwilliams.wales
I network and promote you to my own CW Global Sparks group, my **LinkedIn, Instagram, Facebook and Twitter networks.**
I look forward to my conversation with YOU on The Carolyn Williams Show.
Zoom Details will be sent to you when you decide which dates on Tuesdays and Fridays are suitable to you GMT and global times.

Carolyn Williams is inviting you to a scheduled Zoom meeting.

Topic: Carolyn Williams's Personal Meeting Room

See you in the Live Lounge. <u>Carolyn Williams</u>

Entrepreneur and Founder of The Carolyn Williams Show and CW Global Sparks. A graduate 'speak to inspire speaker' from London Real

Carolyn Williams

Carolyn Williams Defying concrete and healing still, a year later 🖤🙏 22-09-2021

Here's wishing you all a fantastic and safe 2022.

Love from me.
Carolyn Williams😊

CPSIA information can be obtained
at www.ICGtesting.com
Printed in the USA
LVHW051517180422
716475LV00008B/552

9 781783 826247